200 Anecdotes to look smart

(that they don't teach you in school)

Follow us on our social networks to keep up to date with the latest news, share what you liked the most and the least and even to send us your suggestions!

Please feel free to leave us a review on this order.
To find it, simply type "La Bibli des Ados" on the Amazon search engine and rate the book you have purchased. We enjoy reading all of your reviews :)

La Bibli des Ados 

Contents

p.4 - 11 : Science and strange phenomena

p.12 - 20 : Ah America... and its people

p.21 - 25 : Incredible stories !

p.26 - 29 : IT and videogames

p.30 - 35 : The human body

p.36 - 48 : Around the world

p.49 - 54 : Food

p.55 - 60 : Not your ordinary history

p.61 - 78 : Useless anecdotes you're going to love

p.79 - 92 : Our friends the animals

p.93 - 98 : Laws that make you go "WTF" !

p.99 - 103 : United Kingdom, our beautiful country

The Eiffel Tower grows

Each year, the height of the Eiffel Tower varies by 20 centimeters.
It grows in the summer and shrinks in the winter.
This phenomenon well known to physicists is called thermal expansion:
the materials that make up the tower react to changes in temperature.

The sun is shrinking!

The diameter of the Sun decreases by one meter with each elapsed hour. Don't worry though, with its 1,392,000 km in diameter, it's not going to disappear soon.

3 *Earth is gaining weight*

The Earth is heavier by several thousand tons each year.

It is mainly the fragments of meteorites that wash up on our planet that increase its mass. In the vast majority of cases, these fragments arrive in the form of dust.

The ocean is still full of mistery

To date, only 5% of the oceans have been explored. Knowing that the liquid surface represents 70% of the Earth, we ultimately know only a small part of our planet.

Waterfalls under water!

There are waterfalls underwater! They are formed when warm water meets colder water.
And the largest in the world is known as the Denmark Strait and measures 3,500 meters.

Bleach expires

Yes yes, after a year it will not be as effective and will need to be diluted in water to retain its properties.

7 *And you, are you a cow?*

Boanthropy is a psychological disorder where the victim believes he or she is a cow and behaves as such. We don't know if we should find it funny or creepy ...

Clouds are actually pretty heavy 8

A cloud can weigh up to 800,000 tonnes.
It is all the water in a cloud that makes it that heavy.
Fortunately it remains wisely in the sky ...

9 *Achoo ?*

You cannot sneeze while you sleep because the brain stops this reflex.

Planet Mars is full of surprises! 10

Sunsets on planet Mars are blue. This is due to the Martian atmosphere which allows blue light to pass more easily than other colors. A story of wavelength ... does that mean anything to you?

11 *The universe is infinite*

There are more stars in the sky than grains of sand on all the beaches in the world. This can give you an idea of the extent of the universe, which is in constant expansion.

It's freaking freezing

-97 degrees Celsius: this is the lowest temperature that has ever been recorded.
Scientists measured this freezing temperature during a research between 2004 and 2016.
A few breaths of air at this temperature are enough to cause death ... It's not so cold in here after all, eh?

13 Dinosaurs are still here

The probability of drinking a glass of water that contains dinosaur urine molecules is almost 100%.
And yes, these fantastic creatures lived so long before us that they had time to squeeze all the water through their stomachs before they evacuated ... Mmmmh ...
You still have to drink water regularly, eh, it's important!

"Behind blue eyes" 14

People with blue eyes are from the same family!
Or at least, they share the same distant ancestor.
The genes of this founding ancestor would have mutated around 10,000 years ago.
Before, everyone had brown eyes of different shades.

15 Stop crying

If you chew gum while peeling onions, you won't have weeping eyes. Lighting a candle or putting the onion in the freezer a few minutes before cutting it also works.

No need for deodorant in Korea 16

Almost all Koreans do not have an armpit odor. The reason for it? The absence of the gene responsible for these odors: ABCC11. In Europe, 98% of us have inherited it.
And yes, we will have to continue to apply deodorant.

Watch out for UFOs!

In the United States, Chapter 14 of Section 1211 of the United States Criminal Code prohibits any United States citizen from coming into contact with aliens or their vehicles.
The penalty is one year's imprisonment and $ 5,000 fine.

Emergencies are overwhelming ... 18

Each year, more than 10,000 Americans are injured while trying strange sex positions.

19 The baths you will take!

A law requires residents of Kentucky to take a bath at least once in a while. Difficult for law enforcement officers to verify anyway ...

Leave your wife alone!

In a city in Wisconsin, United States, a law states that a man should never shoot in the air when his wife is having an orgasm. Real American gentlemen.

21 Gorillas are fine, but not just anywhere!

In the state of Massachusetts, gorillas are not allowed to sit in the back of the vehicle or you'll face a fine. However, they can be placed in the front seat on the passenger side.

Under close surveillance 22

In Kentucky, women who decide to wear a swimsuit while driving must carry a defense instrument with them or be accompanied by two police officers.

23 *Chickens must stay in the henhouse!*

A law in Georgia prohibits chickens from crossing the road. Chickens with feathers, not those with a blue uniform eh! Otherwise ... it's KFC direction.

Smoking kills!

In Indiana, monkeys are not allowed to smoke cigarettes. That's all we need!

Better not be a California whale ...

In California, it is illegal to shoot someone from your car. Only whales can be targeted.

One sleepless night ? Too easy !

In a scientific study, young American Randy Gardner stayed awake for 264.4 hours, or 11 days without caffeine and drugs.
He still holds the record for the longest sleepless period to this day.

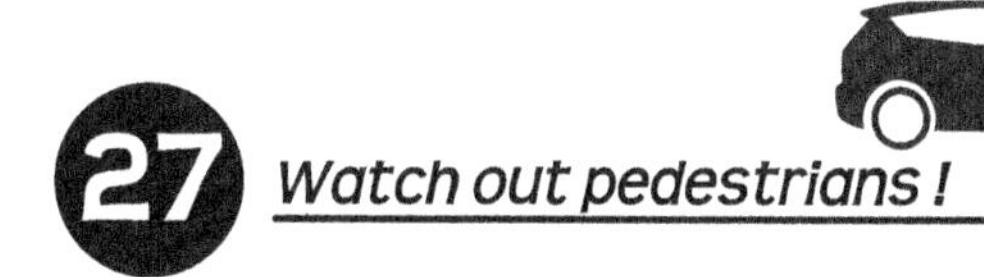

27 Watch out pedestrians !

In the state of Virginia, a woman cannot drive a car unless her husband runs in front of the vehicle, a red flag in hand, to warn pedestrians and other vehicles.

Don't you mess with my hair ! 28

2% of American hairdressers have already been sued for failing a haircut.

Fishing is a serious business

In Chicago, Illinois, it is illegal to fish in your pajamas. So better put on your jeans before casting your fishing rod!

You may sit down

3! This is the maximum number of sips you can drink while standing in the state of Texas. Whoever wants to drink more will have to sit down.
At least there is no risk of falling to the ground under the influence of alcohol.

31 *No need to show off!*

In Illinois, it is illegal to ride a bicycle without your hands.

Hey, do you have any codes for me? 32

In America, using a roommate's or a friend's Netflix account is considered a federal crime. No kidding!

33 *God has no humor*

In Alabama, it is forbidden to wear a fake mustache for the purpose of making people laugh in church.

Avoid going to the hospital... 34

Medical error is the third leading cause of death in the United States. From diagnostic errors, to drug overdoses and communication problems, deaths are numerous.

35 (Not) very lucky !

7 times ! This is the number of times lightning struck Roy Cleveland Sullivan, an American ranger between 1942 and 1977. Incredibly unlucky or truly miraculous? In any case, the man survived all these disasters and lived to be 71 years old.

7 590 020 dollars !

$ 7,590,020 is the sum a buyer had to fork out to win an auction for a US $ 20 gold coin produced in 1933 in only a few copies.

This makes it the most expensive coin ever to be auctioned.

37 *She finds a precious object lost in 1995!*

In Sweden, a woman finds her wedding ring 16 years after losing it ... around a carrot growing in her garden. Luckily, the wedding band set with seven small diamonds was still in perfect condition. The bad thing was, the carrot was so small that she almost threw it away without noticing the wedding ring.

No hard feelings! 38

In March 2019, a New Orleans hotel offered a stay in the Presidential Suite valued at $ 15,000 to the person who brought the most outrageous object ever stolen from the hotel.
Come on... no hard feelings!

39 To infinity and beyond...

In 1982, American Larry Walters attached 45 helium-filled balloons to a lawn chair and rose to an altitude of 4,600m before landing with some difficulty.

A real mother hen 40

In the 18th century, a Russian woman gave birth to 69 children in her lifetime, sixteen times twins, seven times triplets and four times quadruplets. A record.

41 *It wasn't her time*

In 1972, a Serbian flight attendant survived a plane crash after falling over 10,000 meters. She is the only survivor of the 28 occupants of the aircraft.
It still took six months in a cast and a year of hospitalization before she got back to a normal life.

Third time's the charm 42

In 2019, a woman gave birth to twins less than a month after giving birth to a baby boy.
Extremely rare, she had a double uterus which allowed the fetuses to develop simultaneously.

43 Even his own family didn't like him!

Hitler's nephew wrote an essay titled "Why I Hate my Uncle" defaming the dictator and then he went to join the United States Navy to fight him.
Serves him right !

Technical inspection passed

A resident of Calvados in France drives a Peugeot 203, a car she has had since ... 1954! This 94-year-old woman has never had an accident with it and continues to ride and pass technical checks successfully.

Hackers have a sense of humor

In 1999, hackers exposed a security hole in Hotmail (online messaging) where anyone could log into any account using the password "eh".

TheFacebook 46

In 2005, Mark Zuckerberg tried unsuccessfully to sell Facebook for $ 75 million. At the time, it was called TheFacebook.

47 *That's the beauty of technology!*

Selfies are responsible for more deaths than sharks! Some are ready to take all the risks to get THE photo, sometimes even risking their own life. Between 2011 and 2017, an estimated 259 people died while taking selfies.

Amen! 48

You are more likely to get a computer virus on a religious site than on a pornographic one.

49 *Bluetooth, an ancient history*

"Bluetooth" technology was named after a 10th century Viking king, King Harald Bluetooth (meaning "blue tooth"). He united Denmark and Norway, just as wireless technology unites computers and cell phones.

Here we go ! 50

Everyone thinks that in Mario video game, the famous plumber hits the blocks with his head, but if you take a closer look, you can see that he is actually touching them with his hand.

The resemblance is stunning!

If you go back and forth with a finger in your ear, you'll hear the same sound as the famous arcade game: Pacman.

The magic of the internet

By typing the series of numbers 241543903 on Google, you will come across photos of people who have their faces stuck in their fridge or freezer.
The story begins in 2009 when a New Yorker posted a photo of himself with his head in his freezer. He took the opportunity to ask people to do the same thing as him by systematically naming their photo "241543903".
Even today, the phenomenon is still going on ...

53 Your thumb is the same length as your nose

Just like your foot is the same size as your forearm.
This one is harder to verify, eh?

It's tiny! 54

The smallest bone in the human body is in the ear and measures just 3x2,5 mm (0,11811 x 0,0984252 inches).

55 Do you have a hammer?

There is enough iron in the human body to make a small nail of about 7 cm (2,75591 inches). Most of this iron is found in the blood.

Not for the faint of heart

In 1977, a 13-year-old noticed a tooth growing on his left foot.
Once doctors also discovered a tooth growing in the nose of a young 22 year old ... Creepy.

57 *The competition is tough to see the world*

A testicle produces 10 million sperm every day. That's a lot of people!

It's surprising! 58

Human feet are made up of 52 bones, or 25% of all bones in the body!

59 *This organ is full of fat*

The brain is the most fatty organ that humans have. It is made up of about 60% fat.
What a fat fat brain!

It travels better than on the suburbs of London! 60

In a day, our blood has time to circulate around our body about 1000 times.

61 100 000 !

Unless you're bald, you have around 100,000 hairs on your head.

It's fast! 62

It takes 7 seconds for the food to go from your mouth to your stomach.

63 This organ is a real phoenix!

The tooth is the only human organ that can heal itself.

It grows!

Every night our body grows a few millimeters. But this growth is temporary, and we regain our former size as soon as we wake up due to the effect of gravity.

All roads (really) lead to Rome

There is a city called Rome on every continent of our planet (including Europe, Asia, Oceania, America and Africa).
They can be found exactly in Romania, the United States, Australia and South Africa.

We've all been around the world

We take around 7,500 steps a day.
Over a lifetime (which lasts on average 80 years), we walk more than 170,000km, or 4 times around the earth.

Welcome to the island of pigs !

Big Major Cay (also known as Pig Island) is an island in the Bahamas inhabited exclusively by ... pigs. Brought back by sailors as a source of food, they have been forgotten here and are a real attraction for tourists from all over the world.

Chinese people are crazy !

During their training, Chinese soldiers see all sorts of things.
The army trains them to walk with a needle placed at their neck so that they keep their heads held high.
Doesn't it make you want to join the Chinese army?

A little tea to digest it all?

British Army tanks are all equipped to make tea or coffee. Yes, even in the middle of a fight, there is still water boiling! Ah the Brits ...

Vodka makes you rich

Russian love for vodka is no legend! This alcoholic drink generates about 10% of government revenue on its own ... A hell of a lot of money.

The shortest flight in the world!

The world's shortest commercial flight is to the north of Scotland. It connects two islands separated by only 2.7km in 90 seconds.
Not even time to order a drink or eat peanuts!

They don't just make burgers !

In the Philippines, the famous big M fast food restaurant serves its customers... spaghetti! So next time you go on vacation there, are you going to order a McSpaghetti?

73 A flower like no other !

Originally from Mexico, chocolate cosmos (or cosmos atrosanguineus) is a dark red flower that has the peculiarity of smelling like chocolate.
However, it is not edible.

A country the size of a village! 74

The smallest country in the world has less than 1,000 inhabitants. It is the Vatican, the small 0.44 square km state ruled by the Pope.
Latin is its official language.

75 *It needs to be done !*

In 2014, a woman who went missing while on vacation in Iceland wasn't found untill she had been part of the rescue team that had been looking for her.
The woman did not recognize herself when the rescuers described the missing person ...

There is definitely something going on in Iceland ...

At the end of the 20th century, more than 50% of the Icelandic population believed in the existence of the elves.

What the seal ?

Since the early 1990s, dogs have no longer been allowed to roam the land of Antarctica.
This decision was made out of fear that they would transmit diseases to seals.

Cannot wait for the Christmas dinner !

For their Christmas meal, Slovaks place carps in their bathtub for a few days before eating them. At least they make sure the fish is fresh !

One day cats will rule the world ...

A cat named Strubbs served as the mayor of a historic district in Alaska until his death on July 21, 2017.

The effects of pollution can give you some ideas ...

A Canadian company started selling canned fresh air.
It started out as a joke and then Chinese consumers made it real by paying up to $ 20 a box.

We don't know if we should laugh about it because it says a lot about the level of pollution in their air ...

Roll on Valentine's Day!

In South Korea, only women give men gifts for Valentine's Day.
So gentlemen, do we suddenly want to move to Asia?

The world's longest place name

It consists of 85 letters !

Taumatawhakatangihangakoauauotamateaturipukakapikimaungahoronukupokaiwhenuakitanatahu :

This is the charming name of a hill in New Zealand. The name sign is so long that the destination has become very popular among curious tourists.

83 *Ducks everywhere !*

In 1992, nearly 30,000 rubber ducks were lost by a freighter in the Pacific Ocean and are still found regularly today.
This story has helped scientists shed light on their understanding of ocean currents.

No, it's not English ! 84

Mandarin Chinese is the most widely spoken language in the world with 950 million people as their mother tongue and 200 million as their second language.

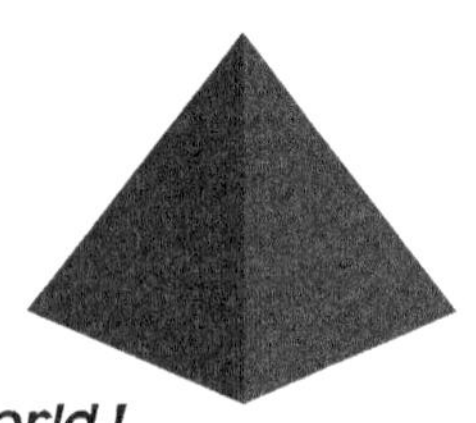

85 The biggest pyramid in the world !

The largest pyramid in the world is not located in Egypt but... in Mexico!
The Pyramid of Cholula has a base 4 times the size of the Great Pyramid of Giza.
It is however less known because it is partially buried under a mountain.

They don't have time in Russia ! 86

The Russians use taxi ambulances. Some unscrupulous businessmen don't hesitate to rent these vehicles for € 200 an hour to take advantage of the sirens that speed up traffic.

87 *No need for GPS !*

London taxi drivers have an elephant's memory! Before practicing their profession, they must study no less than 320 routes, 25,000 streets and 20,000 landmarks ... which can take up to 4 years.

The most printed book in the world ! 88

It's not Harry Potter, nor the Bible ... IKEA's catalog is the most printed book in the world!

The Swedish giant prints more than 200 million copies each year for the 72 countries in which it operates.

No one is alone

When someone who dies alone in the Netherlands, that is to say without relatives and without anyone attending his/her funeral, a person will come to recite a poem during the ceremony.

The country first set up this ritual in Amsterdam, where poets started searching for deceased people to write them a poet in their honor.

There's no need for Google translate

The chief translator of the European Parliament speaks 32 languages fluently!

Now you have no more excuses for getting bad grades in foreign languages ...

91 *A surprising experience !*

Grapes placed side by side in a microwave oven produce a luminous plasma capable of creating some sorts of fireworks!
Please note, the experiment was carried out by experienced scientists and should not be tried out at home!
You could damage the oven or set the house on fire.

Think you know everything about ketchup ? 92

Ketchup was sold in the 1830s as a medicine.
The tomato was known for its benefits against jaundice and indigestion problems.

Apples last for a long time ...

The apples you buy at the supermarket weren't picked the day before, far from it!

They are harvested at the end of summer and can be stored for up to a year in cold rooms before arriving in your fruit basket.

The miracle food for weight loss !

Celery is such a low-calorie food that just chewing it costs more calories than it provides you.

If you want to lose weight, you know what to do.

Dijon mustard does not come from Dijon

Much of Dijon mustard is grown in Canada.

Although it is prepared in Burgundy, its main ingredient (mustard seed) is imported in 80% of cases from the other side of the Atlantic.

Think you know everything about your favorite drink ?

Without colouring, Coke would look green.

The "caramel" aspect has been added to make the drink more alluring.

This fruit is amazing !

Cucumber can fight bad breath.

Besides, you should go cut yourself a slice, it smells good in here!

Seriously, did you know that cucumber was a fruit and not a vegetable as we tend to think?

This incredible statistic on rice !

More than 20% of the calories consumed by humans worldwide come from rice.

99 *It sucks !*

"Dragon's Breath" is the most powerful chili pepper in the world. So much so that it can be lethal ! Whoever risks it can potentially have a burnt airway.

Does water go bad ? 100

The expiration date on plastic water bottles is actually for plastic, not the liquid.

After a while, plastic begins to leach into the water, which does not spoil.

101 *Not all strawberries are red!*

Some varieties of strawberries can be yellow and even taste like pineapple.

Mushrooms shine !

There are over 70 species of glow-in-the-dark mushrooms.
According to scientists, their brightness could help the dispersal of their spores by attracting nocturnal insects.

103 *High five !*

Emperor Shah Khan Jahân of the Mughal dynasty was buried with a hand protruding from his grave so that visitors could shake it.

No time to rest for warriors ! 104

Over the past 3,500 years, there have been approximately 230 years of peace throughout the civilized world.
Well, that's an awful lot of wartime ...

105 *The big jump had to wait !*

The parachute was invented at the end of the 18th century, one hundred years before the airplane. Suffice to say that the parachute jumps must not have been numerous between these two dates ...

1939 - ???? 106

World War II between Japan and Russia is still officially not over.
The two countries have never signed a peace treaty.

107 Christmas in February ?

February was once the last month of the year, which is why it has the shortest number of days.

The new year therefore began at the beginning of spring, which seemed more logical because it is synonymous with renewal.

Hands up ! 108

In the Middle Ages, shaking hands was used to prove that you weren't hiding a weapon behind your back.
However, the origin of this social code dates back to the 5th century BC.

109 7% of all of humanity is alive!

Men currently alive represent 7% of the total number of people who have ever lived.
Since the first Homo Sapiens appeared 50,000 years ago, 108 billion people have been born.
Our current population (over 7 billion inhabitants) therefore represents 7% of all people who have inhabited the Earth.

Mmmh a good rock ! 110

Dinosaurs swallowed large stones that remained in their stomachs to help them digest their food.
Not to be tried at home!

The woman who terrorized the world ...

Probably the greatest pirate of all time was... a woman!

In the 19th century, Ching Shih, a former Chinese sex worker, managed to command more than 1,800 boats and nearly 80,000 men.

She was the most powerful and respected pirate of her time.

The guillotine was not just for men !

In the Middle Ages, more precisely in 1386, in the French village of Fontenay-aux-Roses, there was a trial unlike any other: that of a young pig.

The latter was tried for attacking a baby in the face, which died from his injuries. The pig was sent to jail and later executed.

The defence he provided himself for his crime hadn't clearly been strong enough.

It was common at that time to judge animals.

113 The Romans had perfect teeth !

The ancient Romans of Pompeii had white teeth.

And yet, they didn't use a toothbrush.

No need ! Thanks to their diet very low in sugars, their teeth were naturally well cared for.

The Mona Lisa has been stolen ! 114

Almost no one knew about the Mona Lisa until it was stolen in 1911.

It was an Italian glazier who had worked at the Louvre museum who took it and kept it in a Parisian apartment for two years before being caught by trying to sell the painting to an antique dealer.

115 *We spend years in the toilet !*

On average, we spend nearly 3 years of our life sitting on the toilet sit ...
Women stay longer than men.

Long live the roundabouts ! 116

A person spends an average of 6 months of their life in front of a red light.

117 *Sharks are not that lethal*

More people are killed each year by falling coconuts than because of shark attacks.

I swear by my... 118

In ancient Rome, when a man testified in court, he swore on his testicles.

119 *Currently, 50 million people drink alcohol !*

It is estimated that on average 0.7% of the world population is drunk. Or a little over 50 million people.

Fart yes, burp no ! 120

It's impossible to burp in space.
Indeed, everything in your stomach floats like bubbles full of lumps.
On the other hand, it is possible to fart.

121 *The longest film in the world lasts 1 month !*

The longest film in the world lasts 720 hours, or a whole month!
This film is a tribute from a Swedish father to his son who tragically died of an overdose at the age of 21.

Counting to a billion is possible !

30 years: that's the time it takes for a man who plans to count to 1 billion.

123 *We would have to eat a lot of flageolet beans ...*

By farting continuously for 6 years and 9 months, you will produce enough gas to create the energy of an atomic bomb.

We said no bum on the photocopier ! 124

On average 23% of copier problems around the world are caused by smart kids sitting on them to photocopy their buttocks.

125 *1 in 13,983,816 chance of winning the jackpot*

Dying on a plane, being hit by an asteroid, getting struck by lightning, having triplets or being born with 6 fingers. All of these things have one thing in common: the likelihood of it happening is higher than winning the lotto.

An incredible statistic ! 126

You are 100 times more likely to get an ostrich egg on your head than to be eaten by a shark.
Unless of course you go surfing every day in Reunion ...

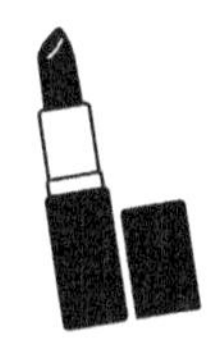

127 *Lipstick is good*

The average woman swallows 3 kilograms of lipstick in her lifetime.

Airplane traffic rules

As for cars, the priority to the right also applies to airplanes.

129 An astonishing etymology !

The word "assassin" comes from the Arabic "haschashin" which refers to people who smoke hashish (cannabis)

Long live DNA testing ! 130

On average, 4,000 newborns are given to the wrong parents each year.
Do you think you don't look very much like your parents all of a sudden?

131 *Achoo !*

You cannot sneeze with your eyes open.
It is a reflex that scientists cannot yet explain with precision.

It is impossible to whistle while holding your nose ! 132

You just tried, didn't you? This is because the air needs to come out of the nose to create the hissing sound.

133 *The end of a belief*

The sound you hear when you press a seashell against your ear is not the sound of the sea but the sound of the bloodstream in your ear.

Mother-son love is beautiful 134

Rapper Snoop Dogg is actually Cordozar Calvin Broadus Jr.
It was indeed his mother who came up with that pseudonym, because she thought her son looked like the character of Snoopy.
That was a nice one, motha!

135 *Condoms under warranty !*

The first rubber condom was invented in 1880 by the Goodyear company.
It was then indicated that the object was washable after use.
The manufacturer even announced a five-year warranty.

Men need landmarks 136

We are unable to walk in a straight line without a visual cue.
Blindfolded, we would gradually walk in a circle.

137 Some lookalikes can be very similar !

Charlie Chaplin came third in a lookalike contest... of himself!

A brilliant idea ! 138

The cotton candy machine was invented at the beginning of the 20th century by... a dentist! Clever isn't it?

139 *Mosquitoes can kill us but ...*

Before mosquitoes can drain us of all our blood, there is much work to be done ... It would take more than a million of them to bite us simultaneously to pump all our blood.

An atypical professional career

Pope Francis was a nightclub bouncer in his youth. Can you imagine the Pope on a dancefloor?

141 *Sunglasses had another use*

Originally, sunglasses were designed to hide the facial expression of Chinese judges during court sessions.

The world is big ... 142

The entire population of the Earth could enter the city of Los Angeles!
Although the planet has more than 7 billion inhabitants, all would fit in the city of angels standing shoulder to shoulder.

143 *The origin of the roller coaster*

The first roller coasters were used to transport coal.
Seeing how fast they could be, tourists started paying pennies to get in.
Then it became the flagship ride of all amusement parks.

Slovakia, Slovenia ... it's the same, isn't it ? 144

People so often confuse Slovakia and Slovenia that employees from these two countries meet every month to exchange letters that were addressed to the other.

145 *Oh my God !*

the "OMG" acronym, used everywhere these days, is not as recent as you might think.
It was first written by a British admiral in a letter to a certain Wiston Churchill in 1917 during the First World War.

We want some saliva over here ! 146

Over the course of your life, you will produce enough saliva to fill 50 bathtubs.
On average, a human being produces 30 ml (0,105585 ounces) of saliva per hour, which is equivalent to 19,000 liters (4179 gallons) over a life of 72 years!

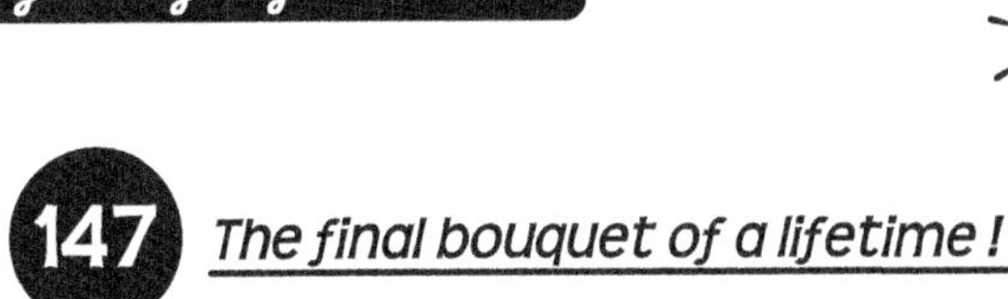

147 *The final bouquet of a lifetime !*

There are companies who offer to use deceased people's ashes to make ... fireworks.
This is called ending in style!

This fruit has 50% of genes in common with humans 148

Man shares 50% of his DNA with ... bananas!

Now we can understand better why this fruit is so good for our health. But that's nothing compared to the pigs with whom we share 90% of our DNA.

So when you call someone a "pig" ... you might not be wrong ;)

149 *Say "cheese" !*

Every two minutes more pictures are taken than all mankind could in the entire 19th century.

Gentlemen, wash your hands ! 150

On average during a day, our hand comes into contact with 15 penises.

151 *An infallible technique to stay alive*

To escape the grip of a crocodile's jaws, you have to push your thumbs into its eyes so it immediately lets go.
Obviously, it's easy to say ...

The rat reproduces faster than the speed of light !

Rats reproduce so quickly that they can have over a million offspring in just 2 years.

153 Bats are all the same

Bats always turn to their left when exiting a cave.

Enduring like a lion !

Lions can mate up to 50 times a day, hot pants!
We wonder when they find the time to hunt ...

155 *The ants have big muscles ...*

Ants are incredibly powerful: they can carry anywhere from 10 to 100 times their weight, depending on the species.

... and are very, very numerous ! 156

There are 1 million ants for every person in the world.

157 *No aperitif for the scorpions !*

A few drops of alcohol on a scorpion are enough to drive them crazy, even stinging themselves and killing themselves.

Whales are very well hung ... 158

A male whale's penis can reach up to 2.5m in length!

And when it ejaculates, it is several tens of liters of semen that it projects ...

Still want to go to the beach this summer?

159 *The dolphin never sleeps !*

The dolphin is forced to stay active in order to breathe.
To sleep, he keeps half of his brain awake.
At this point he is almost still or swimming very slowly.

The Olympic Games for chickens !

The longest flight of a hen on record is 91.9 meters in 13 seconds.
Which is a feat for this species not adapted to fly.

161 *The starfish is amazing !*

A starfish has neither a head nor a brain. If she loses an arm, she can regenerate it.

What a blast, to be a pig ! 162

The pig's orgasm lasts 30 minutes!
We now know why people with a dirty mind might get called "pigs".

163 The chameleon, a hunter unlike any other

A chameleon's tongue is twice the length of its body.
Thanks to it and its speed, the animal manages to catch its prey.

The sloth can live without breathing ! 164

The sloth is able to hold its breath for almost 40 minutes.
Even if your parents say you are lazy, don't try!

165 *This feature makes the elephant unique !*

Elephants are the only animals that are unable to jump.

Are your ankles fine ? 166

The flamingos do not bend their knees but their ankles.
The knees are located so high that they are generally not visible.
This feature allows them to be incredibly stable and to stand up even when sleeping.

167 *A giraffe's tongue is really long !*

A giraffe is able to lick its own ears.
And you, have you already tried?

Octopuses and squids have 3 hearts ! 168

Octopuses have two gills, and two hearts attached to each gill.
It has also a third heart, which is its main one.

169 Snakes are diviners!

According to Chinese researchers, snakes have the ability to predict earthquakes at a distance of 120km up to 5 days before the first tremors hit.

A whale's tongue weighs a lot ... 170

The tongue of the blue whale can weigh as much as an ... elephant, just that!
Indeed, it weighs on average 2.7 tonnes and can even reach 4 tonnes in the strongest specimens.

171 Kangaroos have no size limit!

One fascinating thing about Kangaroos is that they continue to grow until they die.

Fortunately, they don't live more than 25 years.

With iguanas, it's never 2 without 3 ! 172

Iguanas have three eyes.

Two "normal" eyes and a third one on the top of their head which they use to perceive the luminosity.

173 *Sleep like a ... snail !*

We say “sleep like a log” but we should rather say “sleep like a desert snail”.

This snail species holds the record for the longest sleep in the animal kingdom.

It can sleep for up to 3 years until outside temperatures are favorable.

A jellyfish cannot die ! 174

One species of jellyfish is considered immortal. It has the peculiarity of reversing the aging process and cannot die unless it is killed.

175 *Off we go !*

Cows that listen to quiet music produce more milk!

Music has been shown to calm cows and make them more productive as long as the tempo of the music is rather slow.

The dog is the most ruthless predator 176

The deadliest predator is not the lion nor the wolf, but the African wild dog.

According to researchers, the latter manages to kill about 85% of its targets, against only 18% for lions or even 30% for cats.

177 *Poop visible from space !*

The poop of the Adelie penguins can be seen from space.

They love the prawns that live in the cold waters of Antarctica so much that their droppings turn pink.

No need to get on a rocket to check the phenomenon, the pink spots are visible on Google Map.

Crocodiles are real monkeys ! 178

Crocodiles are able to climb trees.

So if you come across one... do not start climbling, instead... run!

However, if they do this, it is usually for the purpose of regulating their internal temperature.

179 Better to avoid solitary pleasures in this country

in Indonesia, male masturbation is punishable by death.
And not in any way: by beheading!

Avoid listening to rap in Uganda ...

In Uganda, it is forbidden to listen to music of erotic or sexual nature.

181 *Let it pass !*

In the United Arab Emirates, the camel has priority on the road. Indeed, the animal is highly respected as a social symbol.

Better be faithful in Hong Kong!

In Hong Kong, a woman can kill her husband (as well as his mistress) to punish him for his infidelity. She will have to do it with her bare hands. The cuckold man has the right to murder his wife however he wants.

183 *An unsuspected weapon ...*

In Germany, a pillow is considered a passive weapon, that is, used to protect against an aggressor.

A full-time job ! 184

On the island of Guam, an archipelago located in the Pacific Ocean, men are paid to deflower virgin women.
In fact, unlike many other countries, it is forbidden to marry as a virgin woman.

185 *It is possible to kill under one condition !*

In the UK it is legal to kill a Scotsman providing he is carrying a bow and arrows.

Everything is allowed in the car ! 186

In Germany, naked driving is allowed because the car is considered a private place.

However, it is strongly recommended to wear shoes, because otherwise insurance does not cover damage in the event of an accident.

187 Animal welfare is essential !

In Switzerland, it is illegal to own a single guinea pig.

He must have at least one companion so that he does not get depressed.

Beijing Express ! 188

In China, tourists are not allowed to drive a car because their licenses are not recognized by the state.

They must therefore systematically hire a car with a driver.

189 In the Philippines, it is better to have 2 cars !

In the Philippines, driving on Mondays is prohibited if your license plate ends with a 1 or 2.

If it begins with a 3 or 4, it's prohibited on Tuesday and so on ...

A reflex to adopt ! 190

In Denmark, it is strictly forbidden to start your car without having checked that no one is underneath.

191 But what are the tourists doing ?

In London, the tube line that connects Leicester Square to Covent Garden is the most popular with tourists, although it is actually faster to cover this distance on foot!

London world tour

The 409 escalators of the London Underground cover a distance equivalent to several trips around the world every week!

193 *1 minute of silence + 1*

Established after the Second World War in the United Kingdom, it is not one but two minutes of silences that are respected: one for the deceased and one for the survivors.

Tea, please ! 194

The English are tea addicts: we drink more tea in England than in any other country (about twenty times more than in the United States).

195 *This castle is quite comfortable !*

Windsor Castle is the oldest continuously inhabited royal residence since it was built nearly a millennium ago in 1070.

Are ghosts naked? 196

Buckingham Palace was built in 1702 on the site of an infamous brothel.

Ding dong !

Contrary to popular belief that Big Ben refers to the world famous clock, this is actually the name of the 13 ton bell.

The tower itself is called St. Stephen's Tower.

London is home to everyone ! 198

London is one of the cities with the greatest cultural diversity in the world, and for good reason: around 25% of Londoners were not born in England!

199 *London: the city of many names.*

Did you know that London has had many names in the past?

It was called Londinium during the Roman invasion, Lundenwic during the Saxon era and Lundenburg during the reign of Alfred the Great.

"London Bridge is falling down" 200

The rhyme "London Bridge is falling down" is known around the world.

Did you know that this rhyme may be over a thousand years old? The Saxons brought down London Bridge using boats and ropes.

People think this is how the nursery rhyme was born.

Printed in Great Britain
by Amazon

72891115R00059